TO A

very special

grandmother

x

LITTLE TIGER GIFT
An imprint of LITTLE TIGER PRESS
1 The Coda Centre, 189 Munster Road, London SW6 6AW
www.littletigerpress.com

First published in Great Britain 2013

Text by Josephine Collins, copyright © Little Tiger Press 2013
Illustrations copyright © Jill Latter 2013
Jill Latter has asserted her right to be identified as the illustrator
of this work under the Copyright, Designs and Patents Act, 1988

A CIP catalogue record for this book is available from the British Library

Printed in China • LTP/1800/0504/1012

10 9 8 7 6 5 4 3 2 1

TO A
very special
grandmother

✗

I *love* the SPECIAL times we have –

just the two of us together.

I feel so LUCKY to have you as my grandmother

and my *friend*.

I *hope*, one day, I will be just like you –

wise and kind, and lots and lots of FUN!

For planning the BEST surprises,

for taking me out on adventures,

for making each moment feel *magical*...

thank you!

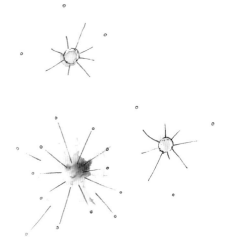

If EVER I'm feeling *sad*,

a HUG with you makes *everything* better!

I *love* to spoil you,

and make you SMILE!

Grandmother, you are...

so calm, so *elegant*,

so sophisticated –

and yet sometimes so full of MISCHIEF!

All grandmothers are *special*...

but you are the BEST!

When it's time to *party*,

you know how to CELEBRATE in style!

I *love* being able to tell you my secrets...

I can talk to you about ANYTHING.

My WONDERFUL grandmother,

when we're apart,

I *miss you* so much.

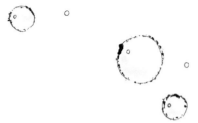

You are BRILLIANT at making

everyone around you *smile*!

For ALWAYS welcoming me with cakes and treats,

and kisses and hugs...

thank you, lovely Gran!

On a HECTIC day,

a quiet cup of tea with you

is the *best* thing in the world.

You *ALWAYS* know how to make me *laugh*!

When things go wrong,

you're the BEST at telling me –

"don't you worry, *better* days will come!"

For *all* the things you've taught me,

for *all* the happy times we've shared...

THANK YOU, Gran – I *love you* so much!

believe I can do ANYTHING!

You *always* make time to listen.

You *always* know just what to say.

You're so very SPECIAL – in all ways – to me!